SARANE ALEXANDRIAN

PIETER BRUEGHEL

THE ELDER

TRANSLATED FROM THE FRENCH BY
ANNE ROSS

basic art library
CROWN PUBLISHERS INC. NEW YORK

Library of Congress Catalog Card Number: 70-87937

Printed in Italy - © 1969 by Ufficipress, S.A. Lugano

All Rights in the U.S.A. are reserved by Crown Publishers Inc., New York., N.Y.

BRUEGHEL

Although he was once nicknamed Brueghel the Joker, then Brueghel of the Peasants, because of his maliciously witty ideas and his liking for rustic scenes, Pieter Brueghel the Elder cannot be limited by definition to one speciality in which he excelled. His originality was so complex that it deserves to be considered from all its varied angles. One can classify him as the true inventor of the genre picture in Flemish painting, as the creator of exuberantly imaginative, allegorical fantasies, as an especially fervent and intuitive interpreter of nature or as the innovator of a plastic orthography which made composition secondary to movement. One could equally well admire him as a thinker who translated his moral philosophy into concrete forms and even as an involved artist who alluded indirectly to current events, that is, to the disturbances in the Netherlands during the Spanish occupation and the religious crisis of the Reformation. He was a potent harbinger of future developments in several fields and the supreme quality of his work consisted in the blending of the multifarious aspects of his personality and the reconciliation of their varied potentials, thanks to the harmony and coherence of his style.

Nothing is known of his origins nor of the circumstances which started him on his vocation as a painter. He was born between 1525 and 1530 in the village of Brueghel, from which he took his name. This village has not been identified, though it may have been Groote-Brogel, near Brée in Belgium, or Brueghel-Son near Eindhoven in Holland, neither is there any definite evidence of whether he came of peasant stock, as was originally thought to be the case, or from a noble family, which later opinion maintained. While still quite young he went to Antwerp, where he seems to have been a pupil of Pieter Coecke van Aelst, who was not only a painter, but an architect, sculptor and designer of stained-glass windows as well. This artist, who was enamoured with Italian art, hardly influenced Brueghel, who learned from him the technique of painting in oils and distemper without acquiring his master's taste for decorative subjects. Pieter Coecke died in 1550 and soon afterwards Brueghel turned to Hieronymus Cock, an engraver and merchant, who kept a shop in Antwerp under the sign of « The Four Winds », and who, being renowned throughout Europe for his dealings in paintings and engravings, was to play an important rôle in Brueghel's development.

After joining the Antwerp Guild of St. Luke in 1551, Brueghel left for the Italian journey which was customary for painters of his time. The dominant

The portrait text within the oval reads:

PETRVS BRVEGEL EX AMBIVARITIS BELGA PICTOR AEVI HVIVS INTER PRINCIPES

PORTRAIT OF PIETER BRUEGHEL. Detail from a Print by Aegidius Sadeler-Spranger

THE FALL OF ICARUS. C. 1558. Royal Museum, Brussels

THE BATTLE BETWEEN CARNIVAL AND LENT. Detail 1959. Kunsthistorisches Museum, Vienna

FLEMISH PROVERBS. Detail 1559. German Museum, Berlin

SHOOTING HARES. Etching

trend in Netherlands painting at the time was that of the « romanists » who attempted to follow Raphael's and Michelangelo's examples, and considered it essential to go to Rome to study classical art. The countless disciples of Frans Floris, the most renowned of the Antwerp « romanists », therefore painted nudes and historical scenes, and despised the exploitation of the resources of nature. From the first Brueghel resisted this fashion, preferring direct observation of

9

SUMMER. Drawing, Art Museum, Hamburg, Germany

nature to academic teaching. During his travels he enthusiastically painted the scenery through which he passed — mountains, meadows, rivers and the sea. He travelled through France (one of his lost paintings depicted the town of Lyon) and in 1553 arrived in Rome, where he met the miniaturist Giulio Clovio, who invited him to collaborate in illuminative work, but Brueghel showed himself less receptive than his fellow-countrymen to the art of the Eternal City. He left for

Sicily — as witness his detailed painting of the Straits of Messina — certainly visited Naples, and returned over the Alps, probably throught the Tyrol. The series of large Italian and Alpine landscapes which he brought back with him have always been greatly admired by collectors. The eighteenth century collector Mariette remarked in his *Abecedario tout* (*ABC of Everything*) the value he put on them, saying: « Titian himself would not have disowned these pen-and-ink landscapes ».

SPRING. Etching after Brueghel

So he started essentially as a landscape-painter and draftsman, and provided with this double foundation constructed for himself a secure career as a manipulator of space. From his stay in Italy he retained no longing to vie with the maestri of the Italian Renaissance. With the exception of *L'Archange Saint-Michel* (*The Archangel Michael*) which does show Mantegna's influence, his later works contain no trace of italianism. His picture *La Chute d'Icare* (*The Fall of Icarus*) portrays no more of the myth recounted by Ovid in the *Metamorphoses* than an impression of a sunny morning by the sea, in spite of the fact that the subject would justify an allusion to Italian art. In the foreground he painted, not Icarus plunging into the waves, but a peasant driving his cart.

On his return to Antwerp in 1554 Brueghel painted some pictures of the Brabant countryside, and became an official supplier to Hieronymus Cock of drafts for engravings. The Antwerp merchant had undertaken to circulating as engravings the work of Hieronymus Bosch, from whom Brueghel drew his inspiration. This influence helped him to pass on from studies of nature to figures. With his drawing *Les Gros Poissons Mangent les Petits* (*Big Fish Eat Little Fish* - 1556) he embarked on the type of painting which was to bring him the title of Bosch's successor. Though he drew phantasmagoric elements from the latter's work, he rethought and recreated them. He substituted for Bosch's mystic lyricism an expression of ironical wisdom which relied on popular commonsense. The following year his series of *Les Sept Péchés Capitaux* (*The Seven Deadly Sins*) confirmed his desire to enrich his allegories with images recalling proverbs or with details drawn from contemporary customs. Thus in *La Colère* (*Anger*) one character is holding a phial of blood, referring to the saying «He would drink his own blood». In *La Paresse* (*Sloth*) a sleeping man is being dragged into his bed by a demon, to illustrate the saying « Sloth is the devil's pillow ». In *La Luxure* (*Lechery*) the main scene depicts a real custom, that of punishing adulterers by binding them to the back of a donkey and beating them while parading them through the streets. This ingenious mixture of fantasy and realism is to be found in all Pieter van der Heyden's prints engraved from drawings by Brueghel, such as the series of the *Sept Vertus* (*The Seven Virtues*), *Le Mercier pillé par les Singes* (*The Haberdasher despoiled by Monkeys*), *L'Ane à l'Ecole* (*The Donkey at School*) and *Le Combat des Tire-Lires et des Coffres-forts* (*The Battle of the Money-Boxes and the Safes*).

Brueghel's work of this period contains variations on the theme of folly, or the « looking-glass world » often used in satirical writings. In his poem *La Nef des Fous* (*The Ship of Fools* - 1495) the Alsatian scholar Sébastien Brandt

THE ADORATION
OF THE MAGI
Detail 1564
National Gallery,
London

THE TRIUMPH OF DEATH. Detail c. 1562. Prado Museum, Madrid

THE TRIUMPH
OF DEATH
Detail c. 1562
Prado Museum,
Madrid

15

HEAD OF A
PEASANT WOMA
1563. Old
Picture Gallery
Munich,
Germany

THE PAINTER
AND THE
ART-LOVER
Drawing
Albertina
Museum,
Vienna

17

had enumerated the various kinds of folly in the world. Erasmus, in his *Eloge de la Folie* (*Eulogy on Folly* - 1511) had written a witty dissertation against errors and prejudices. In the plastic arts Brueghel followed an analogous course, for he held up to ridicule men's senseless enterprises without trying to introduce as

Two Peasants. Drawing, Prince of Liechtenstein's Collection, Vienna

THE TEAM. Drawing, Albertina Museum, Vienna

19

a counter-balance traditional morality, as did the humanists of the Reformation. To make his images more telling and vivid he used the medium of folk-lore, the dicta and usages of which were universally recognizable. His mockery was all the more effective because he pretended to be illustrating episodes from a village chronicle. *La Sorcière de Malleghem* (*The Witch of Malleghem* - 1559) portrays the operation for removing a stone from the head in « Folly Village ». The belief that madness was due to a stone in the head had eventually become a symbolic subject, after first giving rise to a number of charlatans who claimed to be able to extract it. Brueghel used this superstition to denounce the ridiculousness of the Fools, and cruelly stressed the duplicity of the healer and the credulity of her patients.

The best paintings in which he depicted the abnormalities of life date from 1559 - *Le Combat de Carnaval et de Carême* (*The Battle between Carnival and Lent*) and *Les Proverbes Flamands* (*Flemish Proverbs*). One is an allegorical battle, allowing the painter to use the contrast he enjoyed so much between the fat and the thin, and to embrace in a single work the whole yearly cycle of human labour. The other is a universal vision of madness, depicted through those proverbs which showed its existence in the people. Brueghel's love of illustrating Flemish proverbs stemmed from their splendid vividness. It was enough to transcribe them literally into painting in order to obtain the most picturesque effects. All the regional expressions which scoffed at inconsistency and error, such as « Belling the cat », « Talking with two mouths », « One shears the sheep, another the pig », « He is trying to stave in a wall with his head », « He carries a light to the day in a basket », etc. were pretexts for various sketches assembled to form an amazing lexicon of foolishness. It is in these paintings that one perceives Brueghel's meaning, which surpasses art and becomes a humanist reflection.

The content of his work, which often reveals his meditations on the state of the world, has led people to believe that all his paintings conceal a profoundly serious purpose. One of his prints, of a skating scene outside St. George's Gate at Antwerp, has been taken as a symbol of the instability of human existence; a painting of two chained monkeys in a window embrasure overlooking the Scheldt is said to symbolize the slavery of Flanders under the Spanish yoke. Certainly Brueghel's mind was concentrated on philosophical reflection, and could penetrate behind outward appearances, and besides, his friendships showed his cultured outlook. He was in contact with the great geographer Abraham Ortelius, whose atlases were later to revolutionize cartography, and with the printer Chris-

THE PREACHING OF ST. JOHN. 1566
Fine Arts Museum, Budapest

THE MASSACRE OF THE HOLY INNOCENTS. C. 1566
Kunsthistorisches Museum, Vienna

THE TAXING AT BETHLEHEM. 1566
Royal Museum, Brussels

THE TOWER OF BABEL. 1563. Kunsthistorisches Museum, Vienna

CHILDREN AT PLAY. 1560. Fragment, Kunsthistorisches Museum, Vienna

ANGER. Print from the series of the *Seven Deadly Sins*

tophe Plantin, who was a member of a heretical sect to which the painter himself may well have belonged.

Brueghel's intelligence was not however confined to serious reflections. At Antwerp he often visited a merchant from Nuremberg, Hans Franckert, who bought
his paintings and acted as a guide on his excursions into the rustic communities
of the Campine. Carel van Mander, in his *Livre des Peintres* (*Book of Painters*

- 1604) gives the following account of their doings: « Franckert and Brueghel enjoyed going to village fairs and weddings disguised as peasants, bringing presents like everyone else and saying they were relatives of one party or the other ». The same author described Brueghel as « a quiet, steady man, speaking little, but amusing in company », and related that Brueghel enjoyed frightening his companions with ghost stories. This facetious side to his character led him to add

BIG FISH EAT LITTLE FISH. Drawing, Albertina Museum, Vienna

TWO BAGPIPE - PLAYERS
Print from the drawing of the *Pilgrimage of Molenbeeck,* by Brueghel

imaginative features to his ideological views, like the reformers of this time, who were always ready to embellish their doctrines with trenchant witticisms.

In 1563 Brueghel married the daughter of his old teacher, Pieter Coecke van

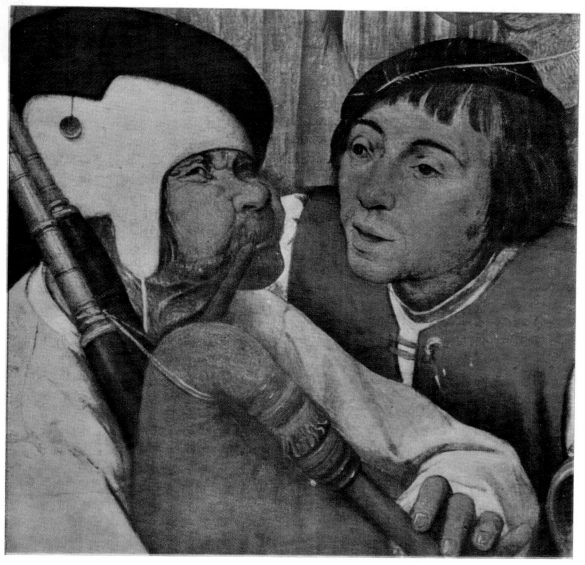

Detail from THE PEASANTS' DANCE. 1568. Kunsthistorisches Museum, Vienna

Two Monkeys. 1562.
German Museum, Berlin

30

THE BAD SHEPHERD. 1565
John G. Johnson's Collection, Philadelphia Museum, Philadelphia, Penn.

THE CONVERSION OF ST. PAUL. 1567
Kunsthistorisches Museum, Vienna

Aelst, whom he had known since she was a child, and settled in Brussels, where his mother-in-law owned an art publishing business. He had now reached the peak of his powers and was entering on a new period, characterized by the amplitude of his artistic means of expression. He could paint a crowd as one makes up a bouquet, mixing similar and contrasting elements. To his draftsmanship he added the charms of a warm, velvety palette, in which primary colours vibrated among the most delicately graded nuances. His genius and his virtuosity were now applied to three parallel groups of subjects: religious — either frighteningly or naturally portrayed; rustic — treating his native countryside and its climate — and subjects which illustrated proverbs or morals.

As a religious painter Brueghel was extremely free in his interpretations, developing his imaginative tendencies in a way which showed how different he was from Bosch, and culminated in *Le Triomphe de la Mort* (*The Triumph of Death*), which he may have painted before leaving Antwerp. This is an epic picture, uniting in a tumult of figures the symbolic theme of the Dance of Death with that of the Horseman of the Apocalypse to create a kind of grandiose poem of fatality. On the other hand, he gave a familiar interpretation to Biblical stories, seeking to involve his spectator in them as in the events of their everyday lives. When he painted *La Tour de Babel* (*The Tower of Babel* - 1563) he was the first to show it unfinished, under construction, so as to demonstrate its technical qualities and give the atmosphere of a building site. In *L'Adoration des Mages* (*The Adoration of the Magi* - 1564) he eliminated any pomposity from the situation and expressed the psychological relationships between the characters.

Among the pictures in which he added topical allusions to a Biblical subject, *Le Dénombrement de Bethléem* (*The Taxing at Bethlehem* - 1566) is the most moving. In treating the subject from St. Luke's Gospel he depicted Bethlehem as a Dutch village in winter. The villagers are killing pigs and carrying wood. The children are throwing snowballs and sliding; on the trestle tables outside an inn the members of the censor's commission have installed themselves and the people are coming up to be registered. In this group is St. Joseph, leading the donkey on which the Virgin is seated, like a modest, anonymous couple blending into the crowd. *Le Massacre des Innocents* (*The Massacre of the Holy Innocents* - c. 1566) is in the same vein; Brueghel has pinpointed the religious drama by transferring it to a local village, with the inhabitants in contemporary dress; the soldiers' red tunics recall those of the Walloon cavalry in the pay of Spain. The emotion was all the more telling because contemporary passions were involved.

THE WITCH OF MALLEGHEM
Print engraved by Pieter van der Heyden after Brueghel

La Prédication de Saint Jean (*The Preaching of St. John* - 1566), conceived in the same vein, was clearly inspired by the public sermons of the Protestant communities; the painter has copied the varied attitudes of a motley crowd drawn from all classes. In *La Conversion de Saint Paul* (*The Conversion of St. Paul* - 1567) the focal point from the religious standpoint (the falling to the earth of Saul and the heavenly light which brought to him his revelation of the faith) is relegated to a secondary place, while the true theme of the picture is the passage of an army through the Alps.

Brueghel's love of nature, which he showed so clearly from his earliest beginnings, deepened into a very full and rich emotion. One might even say that nature with its seasonal variations, the cares of those who draw their livelihood from it and the attention which we are forced to focus on the phenomena of earth and sky, seemed to him the only force which counter-balanced the «topsy-

LECHERY. Engraving from the series of the *Seven Deadly Sins*

turvy world». Man's folly became less important once one grasped the magnificence of the universe and its cycle, which promised eternal renewal. His best client, the rich financier Nicolas Jonghelinck, gave him an opportunity to express this feeling when he commissioned him in 1564 to decorate a room in his new Brussels house with a series of six panels. Only five are known to us, the sixth having either been lost or never painted. They are: *La Journée Sombre* (*The Overcast Day*), *Les Chasseurs dans la Neige* (*Hunters in the Snow*), *La Rentrée des Troupeaux* (*The Return of the Flocks*), *La Fenaison* (*Hay-Making*) and *La Moisson* (*Harvest*). It is not certain whether these were intended as a cycle of the seasons or a calendar, representing pairs of months with their characteristics. In any case, Brueghel here proved that painting was to him supremely a conquest of space. In each painting a road gives onto a panorama of vast perspective, with subtly graded planes which serve as a peaceful backcloth to the work in progress in the fields or to the winter occupations. Though these are fictitious landscapes, bearing no resemblance to any specific place, but combining visual impressions of several different localities, they have a unity and continuity which give the great geographical verisimilitude.

This cult of the earth naturally implied a worship of man. Brueghel's interest in peasants was not that of a painter in love with popular traditions. He sympathized with their work and their pleasures and he had witnessed many aspects of rural life, which he considered the healthiest and most productive of existences. This sympathy is already to be found in *Le Repas de Noces* (*The Wedding-Breakfast* - 1565) in the way he depicts a group of people carousing, but is especially vivid in his *Danse de Noces* (*Wedding Dance* - 1566) and *Danse de Paysans* (*Peasant Dance* - 1568), in which the movements of the bodies and the exhilaration of the faces give a feeling of joy which seems to emanate from the very condition of these creatures close to nature, participating intensely in its most essential manifestations. However Brueghel did not want to idealize his peasants; he always tried to paint them as they were in general, without selecting the most attractive types, and without trying to compose a kind of bucolic vision. The distinction between the beautiful and the ugly had no meaning for Brueghel, who was fundamentally concerned with exactitude. He was spying out significant details, and did not flinch from painting a grimacing face or an unaesthetic gesture if it had a meaning. His drawings prove his passion for truth. Sketched quickly with a pencil, and later revised in ink, they were studies of peasants either front or back view, walking or driving a team. Most often the head is lowered or hidden by a cap or by hair, because he gave less importance to physiognomy

WEDDING DANCE. 1566. Institute of Arts, Detroit, Mich.

PEASANTS' DANCE. 1568.
Kunsthistorisches Museum, Vienna

THE LAND OF MILK AND HONEY. 1567. Old Picture Gallery, Munich, Germany.

THE PROVERB OF THE BIRD'S-NESTER. 1568. Kunsthistorisches Museum, Vienna

THE PARABLE OF THE BLIND. 1568. National Museum, Naples, Italy

Om dar or Diertt is for ougotru
Darr oin oha ir wdmtu

THE MISANTHROPIST. 1568. National Museum, Naples, Italy

The Beggars. 1568. Louvre Museum, Paris

44

than to carriage and clothes. He annotated these drawings with various technical remarks to indicate colours, and usually wrote on the bottom of the page in Flemish the note « n'aer het leven » (from the life). These people were not incorporated into his pictures, and only served as reminders to him. They bore witness to the accuracy of his observation and to the application of his mind to the slightest indications from the outside world.

In his last period the powerfulness of his means of expression, obtained by a skilful simplification of the subject and the processes for portraying it, gave an extraordinary effectiveness to his moral lessons. He avoided rudimentary symbolism and the weighty insistence on an idea. He wanted the moral impression to emerge spontaneously from a naturalistic theme, in the same way as an unexpected sight may lead a man to reflect on the course of fate. *Le Mauvais Berger* (*The Bad Shepherd* - 1565) is a parable from St. John's Gospel, blaming the shepherd who, instead of defending his flock, leaves it to be devoured by the wolf and flees. The flight of the shepherd, whom Brueghel portrays as a large, thickset man, to emphasize the shamefulness of his action, is accompanied by the flight of the landscape. *Le Pays de Cocagne* (*The Land of Milk and Honey* - 1567) is the illustration of a medieval legend about a paradise for lazy gluttons. Here three men from different walks of life — a knight, a peasant and a clerk — are stretched out, replete, beneath a tree where stands a table loaded with food. Nearby, a cactus made of cakes, a roast chicken stepping unaided onto a dish and a boiled egg running on tiny legs to be eaten, make up a picture of an affluent society, so naturally that one has no impression of deliberate didacticism. *Le Dénicheur* (*The Bird's-Nester* - 1568) illustrates the proverb: « He who knows where the nest is has knowledge; he who takes it has possession » (a rough equivalent of « A bird in the hand is worth two in the bush ») but the scene is painted in so unsophisticated and ambiguous a manner that it becomes a topical event as much as a morality. *Le Misanthrope* (*The Misanthropist* - 1568) employs a more dogmatic allegory: a man wearing a black cloak in mourning for the perfidiousness of human nature, is making his way along a road strewn with snares and has his purse stolen by a man in a sphere representing the world. Here again the serene beauty of the landscape gives a tangible realism to the idea.

Finally we come to two pictures which Brueghel painted in the year before his death — *Les Aveugles* (*The Blind Men*) and *Les Mendiants* (*The Beggars*) — which summarize all the characteristics of his moralistic art. In the procession of the Blind, he demonstrates the fate of a group of people going unwittingly to their destruction, by characterizing perfectly each individual and by contrasting the distress of the unfortunates who have already fallen with the self-confidence of those who are as yet unaware of the danger. As for the Beggars, these are legless cripples adorned with foxes' tails, one wearing a paper mitre, another a cardboard crown. They are like caricatures of humanity, their bestial and ostentatious mutilations seeming to parody the impostures and vanities of ambition.

Brueghel died on 5th September, 1569 at Brussels, in the prime of life, being little over 40 years old. He left some works unfinished, notably the pictures commissioned by the town council of Brussels to commemorate the cutting of the Antwerp Canal. During his last illness he destroyed some excessively satirical drawings, so that his wife should not be compromised by them. When he died his sons were five and one year old respectively. Both were to become famous painters. The elder, Pieter Brueghel the Younger, known as the Brueghel of Hell, continued the imaginative tradition of his father; the younger, Jean Brueghel the Elder, called the Velvet Brueghel, developed an original technique for painting landscapes and flowers. One of the latter's daughters married David Téniers, so that Brueghel could be regarded as a founder of a dynasty of painters, all more or less distinguished in the history of Flemish art.

Later, other artists were to follow in the footsteps of the great Brueghel and to interpret in his manner a winter landscape or a genre painting, but none of them could surpass his blazing objectivity and his gift for rendering the characteristics peculiar to a particular aspect of the world universally valid.

Sarane Alexandrian

ILLUSTRATIONS

In the same presentation:

RENOIR   PICASSO
VAN GOGH   REMBRANDT
LAUTREC   EL GRECO
GOYA   GAUGUIN
GIOTTO   CÉZANNE

              DEGAS
              DELACROIX
              CRANACH
              MANET

BRUEGHEL   MONET